THE LITERATURE OF
DEATH AND DYING

SCIENCE
AND IMMORTALITY

BY

WILLIAM OSLER

ARNO PRESS

A New York Times Company

New York / 1977

Reprint Edition 1977 by Arno Press Inc.

Reprinted from a copy in
  The University of Illinois Library

THE LITERATURE OF DEATH AND DYING
ISBN for complete set: 0-405-09550-3
See last pages of this volume for titles.

Manufactured in the United States of America

————◆———

Library of Congress Cataloging in Publication Data

Osler, William, Sir, bart., 1849-1919.
    Science and immortality.

    (The Literature of death and dying)
    Reprint of the 1904 ed. published by Houghton, Mifflin,
Boston, and issued as the Ingersoll lecture, 1904.
    Includes bibliographical references.
    1. Immortality--Addresses, essays, lectures.
I. Title. II. Series. III. Series: The Ingersoll
lecture, Harvard University, 1904.
BT921.O8 1977   236'.22   76-19586
ISBN 0-405-09581-3

The Ingersoll Lecture, 1904

SCIENCE
AND IMMORTALITY

BY

WILLIAM OSLER, M. D., F. R. S.
PROFESSOR OF MEDICINE, JOHNS HOPKINS UNIVERSITY

BOSTON AND NEW YORK
HOUGHTON, MIFFLIN AND COMPANY
The Riverside Press, Cambridge
1904

Published October, 1904

THE INGERSOLL LECTURESHIP

*Extract from the will of Miss Caroline Haskell Ingersoll,
who died in Keene, County of Cheshire, New
Hampshire, Jan. 26, 1893.*

First. In carrying out the wishes of my late
beloved father, George Goldthwait Ingersoll, as
declared by him in his last will and testament, I
give and bequeath to Harvard University in Cambridge, Mass., where my late father was graduated,
and which he always held in love and honor, the
sum of Five thousand dollars ($5,000) as a fund for
the establishment of a Lectureship on a plan some-
what similar to that of the Dudleian lecture, that is
— one lecture to be delivered each year, on any con-
venient day between the last day of May and the
first day of December, on this subject, "the Immortality of Man," said lecture not to form a part
of the usual college course, nor to be delivered by
any Professor or Tutor as part of his usual routine
of instruction, though any such Professor or Tutor
may be appointed to such service. The choice of
said lecturer is not to be limited to any one religious
denomination, nor to any one profession, but may
be that of either clergyman or layman, the appoint-
ment to take place at least six months before the
delivery of said lecture. The above sum to be
safely invested and three fourths of the annual interest thereof to be paid to the lecturer for his
services and the remaining fourth to be expended
in the publishment and gratuitous distribution of
the lecture, a copy of which is always to be fur-
nished by the lecturer for such purpose. The same
lecture to be named and known as "the Ingersoll
lecture on the Immortality of Man."

CONTENTS

Cebes answered: " I agree, Socrates, in the greater part of what you say. But in what concerns the soul men are apt to be incredulous."

Phædo, Plato, Jowett's Translation,
3d ed. II. 209.

" But surely it requires a great deal of argument and many proofs to show that when a man is dead his soul yet exists, and has any force or intelligence." *Ibid.*

Strange, is it not? that of the myriads who
Before us pass'd the door of Darkness through
Not one returns to tell us of the Road,
Which to discover we must travel too."

Rubáiyát of Omar Khayyám.

" Plant one eye of faith in the eye of the soul and itt will utterlie darken with its heavenly brightness the eye of sense and reason, as the sunne the lesser starres."

Diary of the Rev. John Ward, of Stratford-upon-Avon, 1648 to 1679, London, 1839.

"Gone for ever! Ever? No — for since our
dying race began,
Ever, ever, and for ever was the leading light
of man." *Tennyson.*

SCIENCE AND IMMORTALITY

I

INTRODUCTION

N all ages no problem has so stretched to aching the *pia mater* of the thoughtful man as that put in such simple words by Job: "If a man die, shall he live again?" Appreciating the fact that a question of such eternal significance presents special aspects at special periods, Miss Caroline Haskell Ingersoll founded this lectureship in memory of her father, George Goldthwait Ingersoll, of the class of 1805. Knowing that the days were evil and the generation perverse, and imitating, perhaps, the satiric touch in Dean Swift's famous legacy,[1] she made this community the recipient of her bounty.

To attempt to say anything on immortality seems presumptuous, — a subject on which

everything possible has been said before,
and so well said, not only by the master
minds of the race, but by the many far wiser
than I, who have spoken from this place. But
having declined the honor once, and having learned from President Eliot that others
of my profession had also declined, when a
second invitation came it seemed ungracious,
even cowardly, not to accept, though at the
present moment, before so distinguished an
audience, I cannot but envy the discretion
of my friends, and with such a task ahead
I feel as Childe Roland must have felt before the Dark Tower.

One of my colleagues, hearing that I was
to give this lecture, said to me, " What do
you know about immortality ? You will say
a few pleasant things, and quote the 'Religio
Medici,' but there will be nothing certain."
In truth, with his wonted felicity, my life-
long mentor, Sir Thomas Browne, has put
the problem very well when he said, " A
Urn   dialogue between two infants in the womb
Burial   concerning the state of this world might

handsomely illustrate our ignorance of the next, whereof, methinks, we yet discourse in Plato's donne — the cave of transitive shadows — and are but embryon philosophers." Than the physician, no one has a better opportunity to study the attitude of mind of his fellow-men on the problem. Others, perhaps, get nearer to John taking no thought for the morrow, as he disports himself in the pride of life; but who gets so near to the real John as known to his Maker, to John in sickness and in sorrow and sore perplexed as to the future? The physician's work lies on the confines of the shadow-land, and it might be expected that, if to any, to him would come glimpses that might make us less forlorn when in the bitterness of loss we cry, —

Autocrat of the Breakfast Table

> Ah Christ ! that it were possible
> For one short hour to see
> The souls we loved, that they might tell us
> What and where they be !

Tennyson, *Maud*

Neither a philosopher nor the son of a philosopher, I miss the lofty vantage-ground of a prolonged training in things of the spirit enjoyed by my predecessors in this lectureship; but to approach the problem from the standpoint of a man, part at least of whose training has been in the habit and *Ethics* faculty of observation, as Aristotle defines science, and whose philosophy of life is as frankly pragmatic as that of the shepherd in "As You Like It,"[2] may help to keep a discussion of the incomprehensible within the limits of the intelligence of a popular audience.

Within the lifetime of some of us, Science — physical, chemical, and biological — has changed the aspect of the world, changed it more effectively and more permanently than all the efforts of man in all preceding generations. Living in it, we cannot fully appreciate the transformation, and we are too close to the events to realize their tremendous significance. The control of physical energies, the biological revolution and the good start which has been made in a warfare against disease, were the three great

achievements of the nineteenth century,
each one of which has had a profound and
far-reaching influence on almost every rela-
tionship in the life of man. And, not knowing what a day may bring forth, we have entered upon another century in an attitude of
tremulous expectation, and with a feeling
of confidence that the coöperation of many
laborers in many fields will yield a still
richer harvest. It may be asked at the outset whether the subject be one with which
science has anything to do, except on the
broad principle of the famous maxim of
Terence, "Homo sum; humani nihil a
me alienum puto." Goethe remarked that
"mankind is always advancing; man always
remains the same; science deals with mankind," and it may be of interest to inquire
whether in regard to a belief in a future
life, mankind's conquest of nature has made
the individual more or less hopeful of a life
beyond the grave.

A scientific observer, freeing his mind,
as far as possible, from the bonds of educa-

tion and environment, so as to make an impartial study of the problem, would be helped at the outset by the old triple classification, which fits our modern conditions just as it has those of all ages; and I shall make it serve as a framework for this lecture. While accepting a belief in immortality and accepting the phases and forms of the prevailing religion, an immense majority live practically uninfluenced by it, except in so far as it ministers to a wholesale dissonance between the inner and the outer life, and diffuses an atmosphere of general insincerity. A second group, larger, perhaps, to-day than ever before in history, put the supernatural altogether out of man's life, and regard the hereafter as only one of the many inventions he has sought out for himself. A third group, ever small and select, lay hold with the anchor of faith upon eternal life as the controlling influence in this one.

II

THE LAODICEANS

THE desire for immortality seems never to have had a very strong hold upon mankind, and the belief is less widely held than is usually stated, but on this part of the question time will not permit me to do more than to make, in passing, a remark or two. Even to our masters, the Greeks, the future life was a shadowy existence. "Whether they really partake of any good or evil?" asks Aristotle of the *Ethics* dead. Who does not sympathize with the lament of Achilles, stalking among the *Odyssey,* shades and envying the lowliest swain on book xi. earth? "It harrows us with fear and wonder," as Jowett says, speaking of Buddhism, "to learn that this vast system, numerically the most universal or catholic of all religions, and in many of its leading features most like Christianity, is based, not on the hope of eternal life, but of complete annihilation." [3] And the educated Chinaman looks for no personal immortality, but "the generations past and the generations to come form with those that are alive one single whole; all live eternally, though it is only some that happen at any moment to live upon earth." [4]

Practical indifference is the modern attitude of mind; we are Laodiceans, — neither hot nor cold, but lukewarm, as a very superficial observation will make plain. The natural man has only two primal passions, to get and to beget, — to get the means of sustenance (and to-day a little more) and to beget his kind. Satisfy these, and he looks neither before nor after, but goeth forth to his work and to his labor until the evening, and returning, sleeps in Elysium without a thought of whence or whither. At one end of the scale the gay and giddy Cyrenaic rout — the society set of the mod-

ern world, which repeats with wearisome
monotony the same old vices and the same
old follies — cares not a fig for the life to
come. Let us eat and drink; let us enjoy
every hour saved from that eternal silence.
"There be delights, there be recreations and
jolly pastimes that will fetch the day about
from sun to sun, and rock the tedious year
as in a delightful dream." [5] Even our more
sober friends, as we see them day by day, in-
terested in stocks and strikes, in base-ball
and "bridge," arrange their view of this
world entirely regardless of what may be
beyond the flaming barriers — *flammantia
mœnia mundi*. Where, among the educated
and refined, much less among the masses, do
we find any ardent desire for a future life?
It is not a subject of drawing-room conversa-
tion, and the man whose habit it is to button-
hole his acquaintances and inquire earnestly
after their souls, is shunned like the Ancient
Mariner. Among the clergy it is not thought
polite to refer to so delicate a topic except
officially from the pulpit. Most ominous of

Milton,
*Areopagit-
ica*

all, as indicating the utter absence of interest on the part of the public, is the silence
of the press, in the columns of which are
Galatians, manifest daily the works of the flesh. Any
v. 19-21. active demand for a presentation of the
spiritual and of the unseen would require
that they should sow to the spirit and bring
forth the fruits of the spirit. On special oc-
casions only, in sickness and in sorrow, or
in the presence of some great catastrophe,
do disturbing thoughts arise : "Whence are
Shelley, we, and why are we? Of what scene the
Adonais actors or spectators?" and man's heart
grows cold at the thought that he must die,
and that upon him, too, the worms shall feed
sweetly. Few among the religious can re-
proach themselves, as did Donne, with an
over-earnest desire for the next life, and
those few have the same cause as had the
Divine Dean — a burden of earthly cares
too grievous to be borne. The lip-sigh of
discontent, when in full health, at a too
Psalms, prolonged stay in Kedar's tents changes
cxx. 4. quickly, in sickness, to the strong cry of

Hezekiah as he drew near to the gates of *Isaiah,*
the grave. And the eventide of life is not xxxviii. 10.
always hopeful; on the contrary, the older
we grow, the less fixed, very often, is the
belief in a future life. Waller's bi-mundane
prospect[6] is rarely seen to-day. As Howells
tells us of Lowell,[7] "His hold upon a belief
in a life after death weakened with his years."
Like Oliver Wendell Holmes, "We may
love the mystical and talk much of the
shadows, but when it comes to going out
among them and laying hold of them with
the hand of faith, we are not of the excur-
sion." [8]

If among individuals we find little but
indifference to this great question, what
shall we say to the national and public sentiment ? Immortality, and all that it may
mean, is a dead issue in the great move-
ments of the world. In the social and polit-
ical forces what account is taken by practical men of any eternal significance in
life ? Does it ever enter into the consideration of those controlling the destinies of

their fellow creatures that this life is only a preparation for another? To raise the question is to raise a smile. I am not talking of our professions, but of the every-day condition which only serves to emphasize the contrast between the precepts of the gospel and the practice of the street. Without a peradventure it may be said that a living faith in a future existence has not the slightest influence in the settlement of the grave social and national problems which confront the race to-day.

Then, again, we habitually talk of the departed, not as though they had passed from death unto life and were in a state of conscious joy and felicity, or otherwise, but we count them out of our circle with set deliberation, and fix between them and us a gulf as deep as that which separated Dives from Lazarus. That sweet and gracious feeling of an ever-present immortality, so keenly appreciated in the religion of Numa, has no meaning for us. The dead are no longer immanent, and we have

lost that sense of continuity which the
Romans expressed so touchingly in their
private festivals of the Ambarvalia, in
which the dead were invoked and remem-
bered. Even that golden cord of Catholic
doctrine, the Communion of the Saints, so
comforting to the faithful in all ages, is
worn to a thread in our working-day world.
Over our fathers immortality brooded like
the day ; we have consciously thrust it out
of lives so full and busy that we have no
time to make an enduring covenant with
our dead.

Another reason, perhaps, for popular indifference is the vague mistiness of the
picture of the future life, the uncertainty
necessarily pertaining to the things that
" eye hath not seen, nor ear heard, neither
have entered into the heart of man to con-
ceive," the absence of features in the presentation which prove attractive, and the
presence of others most repulsive to the
Western spirit. What is there in the de-
scription in the Apocalypse to appeal to the

Pater,
*Marius the
Epicurean*

matter-of-fact occidental mind? The infinite monotony of the oriental presentation repels rather than attracts, and the sober aspirations of Socrates are more appreciated than the ecstasies of St. John. Commenting upon this Jowett says, " And yet to beings constituted as we are, the monotony of singing psalms would be as great an affliction as the pains of hell, and might be even pleasantly interrupted by them." How little account is taken of our changed attitude of mind on these questions!

Emerson somewhere remarks that the cheapness of man is every day's tragedy, and the way human life has been cheapened in our Western civilization illustrates practically how far we are from any thought of a future existence. Had we any deep conviction that the four thousand persons who were killed last year on the railways of this country,[9] and the nine thousand who met with violent deaths, were living souls whose status in eternity depended on

Plato, Apology

Introduction to Phædo

their belief at the moment when they were
sent to their account "unrespited, unpitied,
unreprieved," — had we, I say, any earnest
conviction of this, would not the hearts of
this people be knit together in a fervid up-
rising such as that which brought destruction upon Benjamin, in the matter of a
certain Levite sojourning on the side of
Mount Ephraim? Think, too, of the count- *Judges*, xix.
less thousands of the Innocents made to
pass through the fire to the Moloch of
civic inefficiency! Of the thousands of
young men and maidens sacrificed annually
to that modern Minotaur, typhoid fever!
We intellectuals, too, bear the brand of
Cain upon our foreheads, and cull out our
college holidays with gladiatorial contests,
which last year cost the lives of thirty-five
young fellows, and brutally maimed other
five hundred.[10] Rend the veil of familiarity
through which we look at this bloody re-
cord, this wholesale slaughter, and a cold
chill will strike the marrow of any thoughtful man, and he will murmur in shame : —

Horace,
Carmina,
I. 35

Eheu! cicatricum et sceleris pudet
Fratrumque.   Quid nos dura refugimus
  Aetas ? quid intactum nefasti
    Liquimus ? unde manum juventus
Metu deorum continuit. [11]

To the scientific student there is much
of interest in what Milton calls this busi-
ness of death, which of all human things
alone is a plain case and admits of no
controversy, and one aspect of it relates

*Eikono-
klastes*

directly to the problem before us. The
popular belief that however careless a man
may be while in health, at least on the
"low, dark verge of life" he is appalled at
the prospect of leaving these warm pre-
cincts to go he knows not where, — this
popular belief is erroneous. As a rule, man
dies as he has lived, uninfluenced practically by the thought of a future life. Bun-
yan could not understand the quiet, easy

*Life and
Death of
Mr. Bad-
man*

death of Mr. Badman, and took it as an
incontestible sign of his damnation. The
ideal death of Cornelius, so beautifully de-

Colloquies

scribed by Erasmus, is rarely seen. In

our modern life the educated man dies
usually as did Mr. Denner in Margaret *John*
Deland's story — wondering, but uncer- *Ward,*
Preacher
tain, generally unconscious and uncon-
cerned.[12] I have careful records of about
five hundred death-beds, studied particularly with reference to the modes of death
and the sensations of the dying. The latter
alone concerns us here. Ninety suffered
bodily pain or distress of one sort or another, eleven showed mental apprehension,
two positive terror, one expressed spiritual
exaltation, one bitter remorse. The great
majority gave no sign one way or the other;
like their birth, their death was a sleep and
a forgetting. The Preacher was right: in
this matter man hath no preëminence over
the beast, — "as the one dieth so dieth the *Ecclesias-*
tes, iii. 19
other."

Take wings of fancy, and ascend with
Icaromenippus, and sit between him and
Empedocles on a ledge in the moon, *Lucian,*
Dialogues
whence you can get a panoramic view of
the ant-like life of man on this world.

What will you see? Busy with domestic and personal duties, absorbed in civic and commercial pursuits, striving and straining for better or worse in state and national affairs, wrangling and fighting between the dwellers in the neighboring ant-hills, — everywhere a scene of restless activity as the hungry generations tread each other down in their haste to the goal, but nowhere will you see any evidence of an overwhelming, dominant, absorbing passion regulating the life of man because he believes this world to be only the training-ground for another and a better one. And this is the most enduring impression a scientific observer would obtain from an impartial view of the situation to-day.

III

THE GALLIONIANS

THE great bulk of the people are lukewarm Laodiceans, concerned less with the future life than with the price of beef or coal. Our scientific student, scanning his fellow men, would soon recognize the second group, the Gallionians, who deliberately put the matter aside as one about which we know nothing and have no means of knowing anything. Like Gallio, they care for none of these things, and *Acts*, **xviii.** live wholly uninfluenced by a thought of the hereafter. They have either reached the intellectual conviction that there is no hope in the grave, or the question remains open, as it did with Darwin, and the absorbing interests of other problems and the every-day calls of domestic life satisfy the mind. It was my privilege to know well one of the greatest naturalists of this country, Joseph Leidy, who reached this standpoint, and I have often heard him say that the question of a future state had long ceased to interest him or to have any influence in his life. I think there can be no doubt that this attitude of mind is more common among naturalists and investigators than in men devoted to literature and the humanities.

Science may be said to have at least four points of contact with a belief in immortality. In the first place, it has caused a profound change in men's thoughts within the past generation. The introduction of a new factor has modified the views of man's origin, of his place in nature, and, in consequence, of his destiny. The belief of our fathers may be expressed in the fewest possible words : "For as in Adam all die, even so in Christ shall all be made alive." Man was an *angelus sepultus* which had —

1 Corinthians, xv. 22

Donne, *Biathanatos*

Forsook the courts of everlasting day,
And chose with us a darksome house of mortal clay.

*Milton,
Hymn
to the
Nativity*

Created in the image of God, "sufficient to have stood, though free to fall," he fell, and is an outlaw from his father's house, to which he is now privileged to return at the price of the Son of God. This is the Sunday story from orthodox pulpits, and it is what we teach to our children. On the other hand, to science man is the one far-off event towards which the whole creation has moved, the crowning glory of organic life, the end-product of a ceaseless evolution which has gone on for æons, since in some early pelagian sea life first appeared, whence and how science knows not. The week-day story tells of man, not a degenerate descendant of the sons of the gods, but the heir of all the ages, with head erect and brow serene, confident in himself, confident in the future, as he pursues the gradual paths of an aspiring change. How profoundly the problem of man's destiny and of his relation to the unseen world has been

*Paradise
Lost*

affected by science is seen in the current literature of the day, which expresses the naturally irreconcilable breach between two such diametrically opposed views of his origin. But this has not been wholly a result of the biological revolution through which we have passed. The critical study of the Bible has weakened the belief in revelation, and so indirectly in immortality, and science has had a good deal to say about the credibility of what purports to be a direct revelation based on miracles. The younger ones among you cannot appreciate the mental cataclysm of the past forty years. The battle of Armageddon has been fought and lost, and many of the survivors, as they tread the *via dolorosa*, feel in aching scars

Paradise Lost

the bitter change
Of fierce extremes, extremes by change more fierce, —

the heavy change from the days when faith was diversified with doubt, to the present days, when doubt is diversified with faith.

Secondly, modern psychological science dispenses altogether with the soul. The old difficulty for which Socrates chided Plato, *Phædo*
Cebes, who feared that —

> the soul
> Which now is mine must reattain
> Immunity from my control,
> And wander round the world again, — Matthew Arnold

this old dread, so hard to charm away, lest in the vast and wandering air the homeless Animula might lose its identity, that eternal form would no longer divide eternal soul from all beside, — this difficulty science ignores altogether. The association of life in all its phases with organization, the association of a gradation of intelligence with increasing complexity of organization, the failure of the development of intelligence with an arrest in cerebral growth in the child, the slow decay of mind with changes in the brain, the absolute dependence of the higher mental attributes upon definite structures, the instantaneous loss of consciousness when the blood supply is cut off from the higher centres — these facts give pause to the scientific student when he tries to think of intelligence apart from organization.[13] Far, very far, from any rational explanation of thought as a condition of matter, why should he consider the, to him, unthinkable proposition of consciousness without a corresponding material basis? The old position, so beautifully expressed by Sir Thomas Browne, "Thus we are men and we know not how: there is something *Religio* in us that can be without us and will be *Medici* after us; though it is strange that it has no history what it was before us, nor cannot tell how it entered us," —this old Platonic and orthodox view has no place in science, which ignores completely this something that will be after us. The new psychologists have ceased to think nobly of the soul, and even speak of it as a complete superfluity. There is much to suggest, and it is a pleasing fancy, that outside our consciousness lie fields of psy-

chical activity analogous to the invisible
yet powerful rays of the spectrum. The
thousand activities of the bodily machine,
some of them noisy enough at times, do
not in health obtrude themselves upon our
consciousness, and just as there is this
enormous subconscious field of vegetative
life, so there may be a vast supra-conscious
sphere of astral life, the manifestations Henry
of which are only now and then in evi- More
dence, — a sphere in which, where all the
nerve of sense is numb, in unconjectured *In Memo-*
bliss or in the abyss of tenfold complicated *riam*, xciii.
change, the spirit itself may commune with
others, " Spirit to Spirit, Ghost to Ghost,"
and do diverse wonders of which we are
told in the volumes of the Society for Psychical Research, and which make us ex-
claim with Montaigne, " The spirit of man
is a great worker of miracles."

Thirdly, the futile search of science for
the spirits. It may be questioned whether
more comfort or sorrow has come to the race
since man peopled the unseen world with

spirits to bless and demons to damn him. On the one hand, what more gracious in life than to think of a guardian spirit, attendant with good influences from the cradle to the grave, or that we are surrounded by an innumerable company from which we are shut off only by this muddy vesture of decay? Perhaps they live in the real world, and we in the shadow-land! Who knows? Perhaps the poet is right : —

> I tell you we are fooled by the eye, the ear:
> These organs muffle us from that real world
> That lies about us; we are duped by brightness.
> The ear, the eye doth make us deaf and blind;
> Else should we be aware of all our dead
> Who pass above us, through us, and beneath us.

Stephen
Phillips,
Herod

If we had to do only with ministering spirits, what a benign effect such a belief might exercise, indeed has exercised, on the minds of men ; but, alas! there is another side to the picture, and there is no blacker chapter in our history than that in which is told the story of the prince of the power of the air and his legions. For weal or for woe, — who

shall say the more potent ? — it is impossible
to over-estimate the importance of this belief
in a spirit-world.

The search of science for the spirits has
been neither long nor earnest ; nor is it a
matter of surprise that it has not been
undertaken earlier by men whose training
had fitted them for the work. It is no clear,
vasty deep, but a muddy, Acheronian pool
in which our modern spirits dwell, with Circe
as the presiding deity and the Witch of
En Dor as her high priestess. Commingling
with the solemn incantations of the devo-
tees who throng the banks, one can hear
the mocking laughter of Puck and of Ariel,
as they play among the sedges and sing the
monotonous refrain, " What fools these
mortals be ! " Sadly besmirched and more
fitted for a sojourn in Ancyra than in
Athens has been the condition of those *Anatomy
of Melan-*
who have returned from the quest, and we *choly*, Part
cannot wonder that scientific men have II. sect. 4
hesitated to stir the pool and risk a touch
from Circe's wand. All the more honor to

those who have with honest effort striven
to pierce the veil and explore the mysteries
which lie behind it. The results are before
us in the volumes of the Society for Psychical Research, and in the remarkable work
of that earnest soul, F. W. H. Myers.[14]
To enter upon a criticism of this whole
question would be presumptuous. I have
not had the special training which gives
value to a judgment, but for many years I
have had a practical interest in it, since
much of my work is among the brothers of
Sir Galahad, and the sisters of Sir Percival,
among the dreamers of dreams and the seers
of visions, whose psychical vagaries often
transcend the bounds of every-day experiences. After a careful review of the literature, can an impartial observer say that the
uncertainty has been rendered less uncer-
tain, the confusion less confounded ? I think
not.

Dare I say
No spirit ever brake the band

In Memo-   That stays him from the native land
riam, xciii.   Where first he walk'd when claspt in clay ?

Who dare say so? But on the other hand, who dare affirm that he has a message from the spirit-land so legible and so sensible that the members of the National Academy of Sciences would convene to discuss it in special meeting?

Fourthly, knowing nothing of an immortality of the spirit, science has put on an immortality of the flesh, and in a remarkable triumph of research has learned to recognize in every living being at once immortal age beside immortal youth. The patiently worked out story of the morphological continuity of the germ plasm is one of the fairy-tales of science. You who listen to me to-day feel organized units in a generation with clear-cut features of its own, a chosen section of the finely woven fringe of life built on the coral reef of past generations, — and, perhaps, if any, you, citizens of no mean city, have a right to feel of some importance. The revelations of modern embryology are a terrible blow to this pride of descent. The individual is nothing more than the transient off-shoot of a germ plasm, which has an unbroken continuity from generation to generation, from age to age. This marvelous embryonic substance is eternally young, eternally productive, eternally forming new individuals to grow up and to perish, while it remains in the progeny always youthful, always increasing, always the same. "Thousands upon thousands of generations which have arisen in the course of ages were its products, but it lives on in the youngest generations with the power of giving origin to coming millions. The individual organism is transient, but its embryonic substance, which produces the mortal tissues, preserves itself imperishable, everlasting, and constant." [15] This astounding revelation not only necessitates a readjustment of our ideas on heredity, but it gives to human life a new and a not very pleasant meaning. It makes us "falter where we firmly trod" to feel that man comes within the sweep of these profound and inviolate biological laws, but it explains why nature — so careless of the single life, so careful of the type — is so lavish with the human beads, and so haphazard in their manufacture, spoiling hundreds, leaving many imperfect, snapping them and cracking them at her will, caring nothing if the precious cord on which they are strung — the germ plasm — remains unbroken. Science minimizes to the vanishing-point the importance of the individual man, and claims that the cosmic and biological laws which control his destiny are wholly inconsistent with the special-providence view in which we were educated, — that beneficent, fatherly providence which cares for the sparrow and numbers the very hairs of our head.

IV

THE TERESIANS [16]

THERE remains for consideration the most interesting group of the three to the scientific student, representing the very opposite pole in life's battery, and either attracting or repelling, according as he has been negatively or positively charged from his cradle. There have always been two contending principles in human affairs, an old-time antagonism which may be traced in mythology and in the theologies, and which in philosophy is represented by idealism and realism, in every-day life by the head and the heart. Aristotle and Plato, Abelard and St. Bernard, Huxley and Newman, represent in different periods the champions of the intellect and of the emotions. Now on the question of the immortality of the soul, the only people who have ever had perfect satisfaction are the idealists, who walk by faith and not by sight. "Many are the wand bearers, few are the mystics," said Plato. "Many be called, but few are chosen," said Christ. Of the hosts that cry Lord! Lord! few have that earnest expectation of the creature which has characterized in every age those strong souls laden with fire who have kept alive this sentiment of immortality, — the little flock of Teresians, who feel that to them it is given to *know* the mysteries. *Matthew, xiii. 11*

Not always the wise men after the flesh (except among the Greeks), more often the lowly and obscure, women more often than men, these Teresians have ever formed the moral leaven of humanity. Narrow, prejudiced, often mistaken in worldly ways and methods, they alone have preserved in the past, and still keep for us to-day, the faith that looks through death. Children of Light, children of the Spirit, whose ways are foolishness to the children of this world, mystics, idealists, with no strong reason for the faith that is in them, yet they compel admiration and imitation by the character of the life they lead and the beneficence of the influence they exert. The serene faith of Socrates with the cup of hemlock at his lips, the heroic devotion of a St. Francis or a St. Teresa, but more often for each one of us the beautiful life of some good woman whose —

In Memo-
riam, xxxii

> Eyes are homes of faithful prayer,
>
> .   .   .   .
>
> Whose loves in higher love endure,

do more to keep alive among the Laodiceans a belief in immortality than all the preaching in the land. Some of you may recall how strongly this is brought out in Cardinal Newman's University Sermon, " Personal Influence, the Means of Propagating the Truth." [17]

Though a little flock, this third group is the salt of the earth, so far as preserving for us a firm conviction of the existence of another and a better world. Not by the lips, but by the life, are men influenced in their beliefs; and when reason calls in vain and arguments fall on deaf ears, the still small voice of a life lived in the full faith of another may charm like the lute of Orpheus and compel an unwilling assent by a strong, indefinable attraction, not to be explained in words, outside the laws of philosophy, — a something which is not apparent to the senses, and which is manifest only in its effects. In that most characteristic Eastern scene before King Darius, in the discussion, Which is the strongest thing in the world, Zorobabel was right in giving woman the preëminence, since she is the incarnation of the emotional, — of that element in life which sways like a reed the minds of men. *1 Esdras, iv.*

The remarkable development of the material side of existence may make us feel that Reason is King, with science as the prime minister, but this is a most short-sighted view of the situation. To-day as always

the heart controls, not alone the beliefs,
but the actions of men, in whose life the
head counts for little, partly because so few
are capable of using their faculties, but
more particularly because we are under the
dominion of the emotions, and our deeds
are the outcome of passion and prejudice,
of sentiment and usage much more than
of reason. From the standpoint of science,
representing the head, there is an irreconcilable hostility to this emotional or cardiac
side of life's problems, yet as one of the
most important facts in man's history it
has to be studied, and has been studied
in a singularly lucid way in this University by one recognized everywhere as a
master in Israel. Unfortunately, with the
heart man believeth, not alone unto right-
eousness, but unto every possible vagary,
from Apollonius of Tyana to Joseph Smith.
Where is the touchstone to which a man
may bring his emotions to the test, when
as the great Stagyrite remarks, ordinary
opinions are not less firmly held by some

William
James

Ethics

than positive knowledge by others? In our temporizing days man is always seeking a safe middle ground between loyalty to the intellectual faculty and submission to authority in an unreasoning acceptance of the things of the spirit. On the question of immortality the only enduring enlightenment is through faith. "Only believe," and "he that believeth," — these are the commandments with comfort; not "only think," and "he that reasoneth," for these are the commandments of science. To many the awkwardness of the mental predicament would be more keenly felt were it not for the subtleness and suppleness of our understanding, which is double and Montaigne diverse, just as the matters are double and diverse.

Though his philosophy finds nothing to support it, at least from the standpoint of Terence the scientific student should be ready to acknowledge the value of a belief in a hereafter as an asset in human life. In the presence of so many mysteries which

have been unveiled, in the presence of so
many yet unsolved, he cannot be dogmatic
and deny the possibility of a future state ;
and however distressing such a negative attitude of mind to the Teresian, like Pyrrho,
he will ask to be left, reserving his judgment, but still inquiring. He will recognize
that amid the turbid ebb and flow of human
misery, a belief in the resurrection of the
dead and the life of the world to come is
the rock of safety to which many of the
noblest of his fellows have clung; he will
gratefully accept the incalculable comfort
of such a belief to those sorrowing for precious friends hid in death's dateless night ;
he will acknowledge with gratitude and
reverence the service to humanity of the
great souls who have departed this life in
a sure and certain hope — but this is all.
Whether across death's threshold we step
from life to life, or whether we go whence
Job, x. 21, we shall not return, even to the land of
22   darkness, as darkness itself, he cannot tell.
Nor is this strange. Science is organized

knowledge, and knowledge is of things we see. Now the things that are seen are temporal; of the things that are unseen science knows nothing, and has at present no means of knowing anything.

The man of science is in a sad quandary to-day. He cannot but feel that the emotional side to which faith leans makes for all that is bright and joyous in life. Fed on the dry husks of facts, the human heart has a hidden want which science cannot supply; as a steady diet it is too strong and meaty, and hinders rather than promotes harmonious mental metabolism. In illustration, what a sad confession that *Autobiography* emotional Dryasdust, Herbert Spencer, has made when he admits that he preferred a third-rate novel to Plato and that he could not read Homer! Extremes meet. The great idealist would have banished poets from his Republic as teachers of myths and fables, and had the apostle of evolution been dictator of a new Utopia, his Index Expurgatorius would have been

still more rigid. To keep his mind sweet
the modern scientific man should be satu-
rated with the Bible and Plato, with Homer,
Shakespeare, and Milton ; to see life through
their eyes may enable him to strike a bal-
ance between the rational and the emotional, which is the most serious difficulty
of the intellectual life.

A word in conclusion to the young men
in the audience. As perplexity of soul will
be your lot and portion, accept the situation
with a good grace. The hopes and fears
which make us men are inseparable, and
this wine-press of Doubt each one of you
must tread alone. It is a trouble from
which no man may deliver his brother or
make agreement with another for him. Better that your spirit's bark be driven far
Shelley, *Adonais* from the shore — far from the trembling
throng whose sails were never to the tem-
pest given — than that you should tie it
up to rot at some lethean wharf. On the
question before us wide and far your hearts
will range from those early days when

matins and evensong, evensong and matins
sang the larger hope of humanity into your
young souls. In certain of you the changes
and chances of the years ahead will reduce
this to a vague sense of eternal continuity,
with which, as Walter Pater says, none of
us wholly part. In a very few it will be be-
gotten again to the lively hope of the Teresians; while a majority will retain the sab-
batical interest of the Laodicean, as little
able to appreciate the fervid enthusiasm of
the one as the cold philosophy of the other.
Some of you will wander through all phases,
to come at last, I trust, to the opinion of
Cicero, who had rather be mistaken with *Tusculan*
Plato than be in the right with those who *Disputa-*
deny altogether the life after death; and *tions*
this is my own *confessio fidei*.

Immortality is a complex problem, difficult to talk about, still more difficult to
write upon with any measure of intelligence
or consistency. Like Simias, in the Golden
Dialogue of the great master, a majority of *Phædo*
sensible men will feel oppressed by the

greatness of the subject and the feebleness of man ; and it is with these feelings I close this simple objective statement of some of the existing conditions of thought.

NOTES

NOTES

NOTE 1, page 3.

"He gave the little wealth he had
    To build a house for fools and mad:
And show'd by one satiric touch
    No nation wanted it so much."
                    Verses on the Death of Dr. Swift.

NOTE 2, page 6.

" I am a true labourer; I earn that I eat, get that
I wear, owe no man hate, envy no man's happi-
ness, glad of other men's good, content with my
harm, and the greatest of my pride " (to paraphrase
Corin's words) is to see my patients get well, and
my students work.

NOTE 3, page 10.

A friend (J. S. B.), thoroughly conversant with
Eastern life and thought, sends the following criticism of this statement : " Jowett's mistake is not his
own. He merely repeats the usual Western error

of thinking — perhaps from the form of the word
— that Nirvana means annihilation in the sense of
destruction, whereas in the East they understand
by it annihilation through growth, in the sense in
which the seed is annihilated in the grown plant,
the ovum in the animal, or any germ or embryonic
form in its complete development. As the possible
development of man is infinite, he is in the same
way annihilated as man by growing to be coexten-
sive with the universe, which is the natural course
of things according to the Eastern view, — the nor-
mal process of growth, which may be hastened
intentionally if desirable."

NOTE 4, page 10.

Letters of a Chinese Official, 1902.

NOTE 5, page 11.

Nowhere is this philosophy of life so graphically
described as in the Wisdom of Solomon, chapter ii. :
"Our life is short and tedious, and in the death
of a man there is no remedy : neither was there any
man known to have returned from the grave. For
we are born at all adventure : and we shall be hereafter as though we had never been : for the breath
in our nostrils is as smoke, and a little spark in the
moving of our heart : which being extinguished,
our body shall be turned into ashes, and our spirit

shall vanish as the soft air. And our name shall be forgotten in time, and no man shall have our works in remembrance, and our life shall pass away as the trace of a cloud, and shall be dispersed as a mist, that is driven away with the beams of the sun, and overcome with the heat thereof. For our time is a very shadow that passeth away; and after our end there is no returning: for it is fast sealed, so that no man cometh again. Come on therefore, let us enjoy the good things that are present: and let us speedily use the creatures like as in youth. Let us fill ourselves with costly wine and ointments: and let no flower of the spring pass by us: let us crown ourselves with rosebuds, before they be withered: let none of us go without his part of our voluptuousness: let us leave tokens of our joyfulness in every place: for this is our portion, and our lot is this."

NOTE 6, page 13.

" The soul's dark cottage, batter'd and decay'd,
   Lets in new light through chinks that Time hath
         made :
   Stronger by weakness, wiser men become
   As they draw near to their eternal home.
   Leaving the old, both worlds at once they view
   That stand upon the threshold of the new."
              Old Age, Edmund Waller.

NOTE 7, page 13.

Literary Friends and Acquaintance, 1902.

NOTE 8, page 13.

Literary Friends and Acquaintance, 1902.

NOTE 9, page 16.

Interstate Commerce Commission, Accident Bulletin, No. 8.

NOTE 10, page 17.

Statistics collected by the *Journal of the American Medical Association*, January 30, 1904.

NOTE 11, page 18.

" By brothers' blows, by brothers' blood,
  Our souls are gashed and stained.
  Alas ! What horror have we fled ?
  What crimes not wrought ? What hath the dread
  Of heaven our youth restrained ? "

(HORACE, *Carmina*, i. 35, Theodore Martin's Translation.)

NOTE 12, page 19.

" Dr. Howe's hand moved slowly back to the big pocket in one of his black coat-tails, and brought out a small, shabby prayer-book.

" ' You will let me read the prayers for the sick,'

he continued gently, and without waiting for a reply began to say with more feeling than Dr. Howe often put into the reading of the service, —

" ' " Dearly beloved, know this, that Almighty God is the Lord of life and death, and of all things to them pertaining ; as " ' —

" ' Archibald,' said Mr. Denner faintly, ' you will excuse me, but this is not — not necessary, as it were.'

" Dr. Howe looked at him blankly, the prayer-book closing in his hand.

" ' I mean,' Mr. Denner added, ' if you will allow me to say so, the time for — for speaking thus has passed. It is now, with me, Archibald.'

" There was a wistful look in his eyes as he spoke.

" ' I know,' answered Dr. Howe tenderly, thinking that the Visitation of the Sick must wait, ' but God enters into now; the Eternal is our refuge, a very present help in time of trouble.'

" ' Ah — yes,' said the sick man ; ' but I should like to approach this from our usual — point of view, if you will be so good. I have every respect for your office, but would it not be easier for us to speak of — of this as we have been in the habit of speaking on all subjects, quite — in our ordinary way, as it were ? You will pardon me, Archibald, if I say anything else seems — ah — unreal ? ' "

NOTE 13, page 26.

This it was which worried Henry More, **the** Platonist, whose treatise on the " Immortality of the Soul" is full of the wonders of the psychical research of that day. " For if we do but observe the great difference of our intellectual operations in infancy and dotage, from what they are when we are in the prime of our years ; and how that our wit grows up by degrees, flourishes for a time, and at last decays, keeping the same pace with the changes that age and years bring into our body, which observes the same laws that flowers and plants do ; what can we suspect, but that the soul of man, which is so magnificently spoken of amongst the learned, is nothing else but a temperature of body, and that it grows and spreads with it, both in bigness and virtues, and withers and dies as the body does, or at least that it does wholly depend on the body in its operations, and that therefore there is no sense nor perception of anything after death ? " (*Works*, 4th ed., 1713, p. 225.)

NOTE 14, page 30.

Human Personality, London, 1903.

NOTE 15, page 32.

Noll, quoted by Beard, *Review of Neurology and Psychiatry*, January, 1904.

NOTE 16, page 34.

Saint Teresa, 1515–1582. In a paragraph before *A Hymn to the Name and Honour of the Admirable Saint Teresa*, Richard Crashaw thus describes her : " A woman, for angelical height of speculation, for masculine courage of performance, more than a woman, who yet a child outran maturity, and durst plot a martyrdom." In another poem he thus apostrophizes her : —

" O thou undaunted daughter of desires !
  By all thy dower of lights and fires ;
  By all the eagle in thee, all the dove ;
  By all thy lives and deaths of love ;
  By thy large draughts of intellectual day ;
  And by thy thirsts of love more large than they ;
  By all thy brim-fill'd bowls of fierce desire ;
  By thy last morning's draught of liquid fire ;
  By the full kingdom of that final kiss
  That seized thy parting soul, and seal'd thee his ;
  By all the Heavens thou hast in him
  (Fair sister of the seraphim) ;
  By all of him we have in thee ;
  Leave nothing of myself in me.
  Let me so read thy life, that I
  Unto all life of mine may die."

An excellent paper upon her life and work, by Annie Fields, appeared in the *Atlantic Monthly* for

March, 1903. In an article, " L'Hystérie de Sainte
Thérèse," in the *Archives de Neurologie,* 1902, Dr.
Rouby gives an analysis of her life and writings
from the standpoint of a modern scientific alienist.

NOTE 17, page 36.

" The men commonly held in popular estimation
are greatest at a distance; they become small as
they are approached ; but the attraction exerted by
unconscious holiness is of an urgent and irresist-
ible nature ; it persuades the weak, the timid, the
wavering, and the inquiring ; it draws forth the af-
fection and loyalty of all who are in a measure
like-minded; and over the thoughtless or perverse
multitude it exercises a sovereign compulsory
sway, bidding them fear and keep silence, on the
ground of its own right divine to rule them, — its
hereditary claim on their obedience, though they
understand not the principles or counsels of that
spirit, which is born, not of blood, nor of the will of
the flesh, nor of the will of man, but of God."

THE LITERATURE OF DEATH AND DYING

Abrahamsson, Hans. **The Origin of Death:** Studies in African Mythology. 1951

Alden, Timothy. **A Collection of American Epitaphs and Inscriptions with Occasional Notes.** Five vols. in two. 1814

Austin, Mary. **Experiences Facing Death.** 1931

Bacon, Francis. **The Historie of Life and Death with Observations Naturall and Experimentall for the Prolongation of Life.** 1638

Barth, Karl. **The Resurrection of the Dead.** 1933

Bataille, Georges. **Death and Sensuality:** A Study of Eroticism and the Taboo. 1962

Bichat, [Marie François] Xavier. **Physiological Researches on Life and Death.** 1827

Browne, Thomas. **Hydriotaphia.** 1927

Carrington, Hereward. **Death:** Its Causes and Phenomena with Special Reference to Immortality. 1921

Comper, Frances M. M., editor. **The Book of the Craft of Dying and Other Early English Tracts Concerning Death.** 1917

Death and the Visual Arts. 1976

Death as a Speculative Theme in Religious, Scientific, and Social Thought. 1976

Donne, John. **Biathanatos.** 1930

Farber, Maurice L. **Theory of Suicide.** 1968

Fechner, Gustav Theodor. **The Little Book of Life After Death.** 1904

Frazer, James George. **The Fear of the Dead in Primitive Religion.** Three vols. in one. 1933/1934/1936

Fulton, Robert. **A Bibliography on Death, Grief and Bereavement:** 1845-1975. 1976

Gorer, Geoffrey. **Death, Grief, and Mourning.** 1965

Gruman, Gerald J. **A History of Ideas About the Prolongation of Life.** 1966

Henry, Andrew F. and James F. Short, Jr. **Suicide and Homicide.** 1954

Howells, W[illiam] D[ean], et al. **In After Days;** Thoughts on the Future Life. 1910

Irion, Paul E. **The Funeral:** Vestige or Value? 1966

Landsberg, Paul-Louis. **The Experience of Death:** The Moral Problem of Suicide. 1953

Maeterlinck, Maurice. **Before the Great Silence.** 1937

Maeterlinck, Maurice. **Death.** 1912

Metchnikoff, Élie. **The Nature of Man:** Studies in Optimistic Philosophy. 1910

Metchnikoff, Élie. **The Prolongation of Life:** Optimistic Studies. 1908

Munk, William. **Euthanasia.** 1887

Osler, William. **Science and Immortality.** 1904

Return to Life: Two Imaginings of the Lazarus Theme. 1976

Stephens, C[harles] A[sbury]. **Natural Salvation:** The Message of Science. 1905

Sulzberger, Cyrus. **My Brother Death.** 1961

Taylor, Jeremy. **The Rule and Exercises of Holy Dying.** 1819

Walker, G[eorge] A[lfred]. **Gatherings from Graveyards.** 1839

Warthin, Aldred Scott. **The Physician of the Dance of Death.** 1931

Whiter, Walter. **Dissertation on the Disorder of Death.** 1819

Whyte, Florence. **The Dance of Death in Spain and Catalonia.** 1931

Wolfenstein, Martha. **Disaster:** A Psychological Essay. 1957

Worcester, Alfred. **The Care of the Aged, the Dying, and the Dead.** 1950

Zandee, J[an]. **Death as an Enemy According to Ancient Egyptian Conceptions.** 1960